How to Deliver Presentations Like a Pro!

The definitive guide to powerful public speaking

Wilf Voss

ISBN 978-0-244-34058-2

Table of Contents

Introduction

Are you confident that you are always delivering important messages in a way that has impact and gets your message across effectively?

In a world where professionals are suffering from 'information overload' it is becoming increasingly difficult for an organisation to ensure that they are effectively engaging with their clients, contacts or members. This book provides tools and techniques for anyone who has to present an important message to ensure that they get their message across highly effectively. The book has a wide coverage with training which is relevant for meetings, presentations and press and public relations. The book is built on many years of practical experience and aims to share professional techniques which can be employed by any professional who needs to communicate effectively.

About the author

Wilf Voss is a highly experienced business consultant and trainer with many years' experience in marketing, event management and customer service.

Over the last twenty years Wilf has given many thousands of presentations to a variety of audiences, from conference hosting to high profile product launches and international awards events he has given numerous interviews for the media.

Wilf's background includes the development and delivery of major events and marketing campaigns worldwide as well as the roles within the London 2012 Olympics and management within major retail organisations.

He has managed and delivered comprehensive mystery shopping programmes and delivered coaching and training to all levels of staff and management.

He has used his experience to develop a series of techniques which encompass marketing, presentation techniques, psychology and theatre to ensure that presentations are second to none ensuring that audiences are both delighted and informed. His techniques can be employed in all environments which require highly effective communication.

Today his skills are called upon as a host and presenter for conferences and events across the UK and internationally and he is also a skilled trainer and coach.

Introduction

This book covers a variety of topics related to the various forms of communication that you require in your organisation.

The book has been set out as a very practical guide. It builds on years of experience and should offer you a shortcut to some professional techniques which will supercharge your meetings, presentations and public relations

You should walk away from this book with a series of tools and techniques which you can use every day and useful checklists and references which you can easily refer to in the future.

Who is this book aimed at?

The book is intended as an introduction for those who have little experience in these areas, however it will also provide a variety of powerful techniques for more experienced people allowing you to develop and improve your communication techniques.

Understanding Communication Methods

Communication is the method by which we pass information between individuals and organisations. There are a large number of communication methods available to us. Unfortunately, the wide variety of methods means that many people now are reaching information overload, and it is becoming more and more difficult to separate important and effective information from the 'noise' of other communications going on around them.

It is for this reason that it is becoming more and more important to employ highly effective communication techniques to ensure that your messages and information are delivered effectively. Unfortunately, it is very simple to slip into the trap of ineffective communication. There are many examples where a lack of preparation undermines the delivery of the message or misses the needs of the audience, which means that the communication is ignored entirely.

Effective communication needs to be:

- relevant and meet the needs of the audience

- authoritative, believable and trusted

- delivered in a way which presents the organisation or the individual in a professional manner.

This book will give you a series of tools and techniques which will allow you to ensure that any communication you use meets these requirements and gains the best impact with the audience.

The fact that an organisation has always given a presentation to illustrate new products, for example, does not negate the fact that you could consider a facilitated workshop or meeting. It is important for each and every communication you wish to deliver to consider:

- What do we need to communicate?

- What is our audience?

- What would the best way to communicate this be?

If you consider these simple questions and get the right answers you will ensure that you are delivering the information in the most relevant way.

The Confident Presenter

- Introduction to presentations and events
  - What is the reason for events
  - What is the general audience expectation
- Overcoming fear or stage-fright
  - Ensuring that you always have the confidence to deliver at your best
- Having the confidence to present
  - Techniques to reduce pre-presentation nerves
- Breathing Exercises
  - Concentrating on breathing and not your nerves
- Mind changers
- Smile and your brain smiles with you!
  - Using music to drive your mood

- Preparing to succeed (Positive thinking in practice)

  o Dealing with doubt

  o Transferring belief

- Becoming an 'Alpha Presenter'

  o Understanding pack mentality with presentations

- Section Review

Introduction to presentations and events

What comes into your mind when you think of a presentation? Is it excitement, anticipation and interest?

Unfortunately, the answer is very likely to be none of the above. Over time many of us have become subjected to poorly created presentations: pages of bullet points on the projector screen; a speaker who didn't hold our interest; need I go on? Technology such as PowerPoint has allowed us to create excellent presentations; however, it also allows us to create the complete opposite.

We need to understand that presentations are more than electronic files: we actually need to understand a bit about the psychology of presentations and learn some secrets which are more common in film and theatre.

Before we look at the presentation tools, we need to look at the presenter. There are two major failings which are identified by people when they see a 'poor' presentation: the presenter and the presentation. We will start with the presenter and how you can become confident, believable and a truly powerful presenter!

Overcoming fear or stage-fright

Does public speaking make you nervous? This is a serious question which you may think has two answers:

- Yes – I am not happy giving presentations in public.

- No – I am a confident presenter.

There is of course a third response, which is that you have some nerves before a presentation but you do not let them hold you back. The nervousness you feel comes from the fact that you are stepping up in front of an audience (often of your peers) and therefore you will need to put your head above the parapet. You may perceive that there is a high risk of failure ('what if they don't like me?') and you may not feel confident that you know what to say.

I would be lying if I could tell you how to completely conquer stage fright. In fact we really don't want to get rid of our stage fright or presentation fear. This is because to do so runs the risk of making your presentation dry or over-rehearsed. In fact if you talk to famous actors they will often tell you that that still have some controlled nerves there before they go on stage, despite the fact that this is their 'day job' and they are very experienced.

It is controlled nerves which will give you an edge and allow you to give amazing presentations. I have given many thousands of presentations to large and small audiences around the world and I can assure you that the day I do not feel that tingle of nervous excitement before I speak is the day I will give up, because I know that is the day I will not be ready to shine on stage.

This book will give you tools and techniques which will allow you to manage any pre-show nerves, and also prepare for anything that may happen during a presentation.

Having the confidence to present

There are a number of techniques to build and support your confidence. The most important one is to ensure that you are fully prepared for your presentation, ensuring that you have confidence in your subject and what you are going to say (we will cover this later in this book). Once you are confident in your subject you are a long way towards giving a confident presentation. To help you further you can use two additional techniques:

- breathing exercises

- mind changers

Breathing Exercises

It is important to remember the following:

- your breathing will affect your voice and projection - learning to control your breathing will allow you to improve the projection and clarity of your voice.

- your breathing can be affected by nerves.

- you can also control your nerves by controlling your breathing.

You have to consider; how often do you think about breathing? It is an automatic function which we never have to think about; it just happens.

Try the following simple breathing exercise:

- take a deep breath in through your mouth

- breath out SLOWLY through your nose (mentally count the seconds that it takes you to breath out)

- concentrate on your breathing and repeat this at least five more times.

There are two benefits, firstly you will get more oxygen into your lungs and therefore feed your brain, and secondly the act of concentration allows you to think about something other than your nerves. Distraction is a good technique; we use it with children and it still works with us as adults. Force yourself to take a moment and think of something else. This is a simple technique that can be carried out anywhere and at any time.

Mind changers

The second simple technique is the use of mind changers. These are two simple tricks which you can use to up your energy and make you feel better. They may sound very simplistic, however, I can promise you that they are very powerful and can work a treat!

First of all, smile. Even if you are feeling like you really don't want to (in fact, particularly if you feel like you don't want to). Then use a mantra: tell yourself out loud that you are great and that you can succeed in your presentation. Repeat it a few times, be confident and really speak out.

There are two techniques at work here. The acts of smiling (and other emotions) are handled by a lower, more primitive part of our brains. If you physically smile the lower brain tells the upper brain that you are happy. It can help you improve the way you feel. If you support this with the second technique, a strong vocal message, it becomes a very powerful, mood changing tool.

Another thing to use is music. We will see later how we can change an audience mode with music, and it can work for you as a presenter also. Think of your favourite upbeat track, how does it make you feel when you hear it on the radio? Think of a track that you would sing along to in the car or shower (or tap the steering wheel if you are not the singing sort!)

Pick a track that appeals to you and makes you feel happy (I use 'Can you feel it?' by the Jackson Five, however you no doubt have better musical taste!). Good music is great for changing your mood. Look at a good movie; they will use slow mournful music when the action is sad or downbeat. (How does this make you feel?) In the same way, happy upbeat music can make you feel great.

Make sure you are musically charged before you go to your presentation by playing your 'mantra track' before you get ready for your presentation..

Preparing to succeed

Before you start any presentation you need to ask yourself if you have any doubts about it. This is important because if you cannot convince yourself, you will not persuade your audience. Before you start speaking you must believe in what you are going to say...

This is the transfer of belief. An audience can detect (from your vocal tone and body language) when you do not believe in what you are talking about. This can seriously affect the acceptance of your presentation.

You need to eliminate any doubts you may have about your presentation, so you need to be sure of the content and subject area. Think about the old saying 'Believe you will fail and you will.' This is true for presentations, but can also be paraphrased as 'Doubt your content and your audience will also doubt it.'

Becoming an 'Alpha Presenter'

In the animal kingdom, pack animals (such as dogs) have a leader called the Alpha animal; this is the animal who leads all of the other animals in the pack. The same should be true in presentations. You as the presenter should be the leader when you are speaking and be seen to be the leading individual. In this way you have control of the audience and also their respect. You should ask yourself, do you have an alpha role when you are presenting? Do you allow the audience to take control of your presentation or do you have full control? When you consider your presentations you should remember that you should:

- have control of the room – this means that if you are speaking you should look to ensure you are the only one speaking. If audience members are talking, pause and see if they stop. (If not, see the techniques for dealing with difficult people later in the course)

- be in control of your content – you demonstrate that you clearly have belief in your subject

- be in control of your confidence – you should 'own the stage', this means that you do not seem timid or apprehensive about your presentation. (The audience can smell fear!)

If you think of yourself as an Alpha Presenter you will be able to bring together the management of pre-event nerves and belief in a whole attitude.

Section Review

You have undertaken the first step of becoming a perfect presenter, so to recap:

- the presenter is key to the presentation

- whereas we cannot completely remove stage-fright we can control it and use it to our advantage

- thinking about your breathing can reduce your nerves and give you time to think and be calm

- be ready to change your mind by smiling and positive vocal phrases

- use upbeat music to move your mind to a more positive state

- get rid of doubts; have confidence in yourself and your presentation

- be in control – you are the Alpha Presenter

Now, let's move on and look at the presentation itself.

The Three P's

- Introduction
- The secret for presentation success
- Getting the preparation balance right
- Understanding your audience's needs
- What do people expect from the presentation
- What do they want from the presentation
- What can you deliver?
- The crucial questions you must ask to meet an audience needs
  - What do they want?
  - What do they know?
- Are there any questions?
  - Will there be questions?
  - Can I answer them?
- Dealing with questions

- How to effectively answer questions from the floor

- Understanding your audience
  - What is the audience dynamic
- Scripting Techniques
  - What you need is not a script...
- Creating Cue Cards
  - Use of cue cards
  - Level of content required
- Rehearsing
  - How to rehearse

Introduction

In this section we are going to introduce the Three Ps. They are:

- Preparation
- Preparation
- Preparation

This will seem obvious; however, a lack of effective preparation will be the downfall of any presentation. The key word is effective preparation. This is ensuring that not only have you prepared a set of slides, but that you are aware of the audience, the environment and your message. Once all of these elements are in place you will have been well on the way to winning over the audience before you have even stood up to speak!

In this section we will take you through the methods you should employ when preparing for a presentation.

Getting the preparation balance right

On the last we introduced the Three Ps and I told you of the importance of preparation; however, there is a caveat. You do need to get the balance right for your preparation. You may not believe it, but you can be too prepared for a presentation with the result that you come across as stilted or over-rehearsed.

You should ensure that you have taken your preparation steps and that you have rehearsed your presentation, however you should resist the temptation to be so prepared that you know your content and your presentation so well that you seem to be reciting content from memory with no concern for the audience.

You are looking for a stage where you are comfortable with the content and the presentation, you know how you will present and you are aware of the aims and objectives and the points you wish to make. This is the stage to stop. Take a break, you are ready to go!

By all means keep the ideas fresh in your mind, but don't keep going over the presentation again and again; you need it to be fresh for your audience. The impression you want to give is that this is the first time you have shared your presentation with anyone (even if you have given the presentation many times before).

Understanding your audience's needs

The first step in the preparation for any presentation is an understanding of what the audience wants to get out of it. It is important to note that this may not be what the title of the presentation you have been given is. You need to ensure that you know as much as you can about your audience before you stand before them. So, for example:

- **Who are the audience?**
    - What is their level of experience and knowledge?
    - It is vital to ensure that you do not stand up and tell them what they already knew or bamboozle them with content which is too complex. o What is the dynamic? – Are the audience going to be senior

directors or shop-floor staff? You need to consider your content and language to meet the needs of the audience. o Where have they come from?

- o Is this a single company or team or is this a public forum? If they do come from one organisation you can make sure that you use some of their house language (the internal terms and phrases each organisation uses) to show affinity with them.

- **What do they expect from the presentation?**

  - o Do their aims and objectives match the ones you have set for your presentation?

  - o What is their expectation for the presentation? Are they expecting a staid and boring speech, is this what you should deliver?

- **What do they want from the presentation?**

  - Do they have specific items of information which are key to them and which they simply must know about? So many presentations I have seen presenters giving reams of information which people gloss over when all they wanted was a short explanation.

- **What can you deliver?**

  - This is the final vital point. Are there items which the audience would like to have but you just cannot deliver? Perhaps something has not been decided upon or finalised

  - It is important, where you can, to not just ignore these items. Be honest if you cannot talk about something; at least tell the audience

this and the reason why. Tell them
when they will get this information.

The crucial questions you must ask to meet an audience's needs

The previous set of questions allowed us to
discover who the audience were and what they
expected and wanted from the presentation,
however there are two other major areas you
need to review. Firstly, what does the audience
already know?

There is no point in boring your audience by
telling them information they already know,
however you would be amazed how many times
presenters do not ask this simple question. In
fact by asking who the audience is you should
have a much better idea of their knowledge
level.

Of course, this is sometimes not as simple as yes,
they have knowledge of some area or no, they
do not. You may find that you have a mixed
audience or, worst still, people who turn up at
the last minute knowing nothing about what
you are talking about!

How can you cope? Try this three-step plan:

1. Know the audience – Find out who the audience will be, then ask the organiser or even some audience members what they know already.

2. Be prepared – Just in case, it is worth the effort to have a couple of 'background slides' which quickly cover the background to what you are presenting. You can quickly introduce these as a set of 'as you know already' facts or go into more detail if required.

3. Read the audience – Watch the body language. Are they bored or disinterested? Is it time to move on!

Are there any questions?

Are you ready to answer questions about your presentation? There are three things you need to consider:

- do you feel ready to give an authoritative answer to a question which may come up? – Did you need to get permission or authority to detail any of the content within your presentation? Do you have the knowledge and permission to answer the sort of questions which may come up?

- is it the right forum to ask for questions? – You need to consider if it will be logistically possible for questions to be handled. For example, a large auditorium may require a number of people with radio microphones to ensure a question is audible to the audience. Is this in place? Equally, what is the expectation for the event - if you ask for questions from the floor will every speaker be expected to do the same?

- will there be any questions? – There can be a horrible silence which follows a call for questions and none of the audience want to say anything (known in the trade as a 'tumbleweed moment'!). The response to this is to be confident and state that you must have covered the content well.

Asking questions can be a simple and useful way to involve the audience and create a more interactive presentation. If you have answered the questions above, you should be ready for questions. The next step is being able to deal with them effectively.

Dealing with questions

Effectively dealing with questions can provide an excellent element for a presentation, however there are a few hints and tips which will allow you to ensure your Q&A sessions go smoothly:

- use a roving microphone – In all but the smallest rooms you will find that it is useful to employ a person (or people) with a roving microphone. This will allow the entire audience to clearly hear the question from the delegate.

- but - use the roving microphone effectively – Be aware that you need to ensure that your microphone wrangler keeps some control over the microphone. It is preferable that the mic is controlled by a sound engineer (who will fade up the mic when the delegate asks a question). If this is not possible ensure that they switch the mic on before handing it to the delegate. It can be embarrassing if the mic does not work and can affect your 'Alpha Presenter' position.

- beware 'mic grab' – mic grab is when a delegate takes the microphone and will not hand it back, determined to ask more questions or worst still to try to argue with you as the presenter. We will deal with difficult people later in the book, however the best policy is for the mic wrangler to take back the microphone when the question has been completed or to hold the microphone for the delegate. Everyone with a question should be given their chance to speak so it is important to firmly, yet politely, ensure that individuals do not take over.

- repeat the question – repeating the question confirms that you have understood what the delegate is asking and ensures that the entire audience has also clearly understood. The delegate may not have spoken clearly and even though you may have heard you must stop the questions becoming a one to one conversation.

- you should have factored time into your presentation for questions; do not allow the session to overrun. At the required time thank the audience and offer to take any further questions 'off-line' after the presentation.

Understanding your audience

We know who your audience is, we know what they want, however there is one more thing which you should be aware of and that is the audience dynamic.

The audience dynamic refers to your audience's mood and body language during your presentation. It is important to watch for changes in the audience as you speak. You will be looking for signs that they are bored or irritated:

- are they becoming bored? – yawning, shuffling papers or reading something else, basically not paying attention to you or the presentation

- are they becoming irritated? – crossed arms, whispering or talking between delegates, people walking out.

The signs will usually start subtly and then increase. The challenge is to do something about the changing dynamic when you first see it. If it is boredom, is this something to do with you? (Ouch – but we have to consider it!) Try picking up the pace; perhaps try asking a question of the audience with a show of hands or similar to get them interacting.

If it is irritation, and this is generally rare, you need to weigh up what may be causing the issue. Were there any items you were aware of in your preparation which may cause an issue with the audience? Again you may do well to move on in your content or, if the issue is not going away, to close the presentation early.

Generally good preparation will prevent these issues, however you are ready if you have an unexpected issue.

Scripting Techniques

Unless you really know your subject inside out, you will need to prepare some form of script for your presentation. Scripts:

- ensure you cover all of the content you intend to within a presentation

- give you structure and a running order for the points you are going to cover

- act as an aid to your memory while you present.

The only thing a script is not; is a script!

Okay, that is a weird statement, however when you present you should be spending your time interacting with the audience; you cannot do this and read a script. The audience will soon guess you are reading the content word for word and will often wonder why you didn't just send the copy to them and save the time of attending the presentation!

You need to know enough of your content and your presentation to be able to have a few words which you can say about each slide somewhat 'off the cuff'. You have two ways to remember what to say: the content of your slides and your cue cards.

Creating Cue Cards

Previously I told you that you should not have a script; what you need to develop is a set of simple cue cards which cover the main points you want to cover on each slide:

The cue cards should be quite small (A5 index card or less) with clear text. The contents should not be a full script for the slide, but bullet points or facts which you wish to ensure that you cover at this point in the presentation.

Write the cards out clearly (or print using a nice large font you can glance at quickly) and then punch a hole in the top left hand corner and attach them together with a treasury tag. Attaching them together is important – just think what would happen if you dropped them and got them out of order!

You should then place them in front of you (or hold them in your hand) and practice glancing at the contents. This, with the pictures or text on the slide, should be all you need.

Rehearsing

A good rehearsal can be a great way to ensure that you are comfortable with your presentation and script. There are two main types of rehearsal: mirror and in-situ.

Mirror Rehearsals

They are called mirror rehearsals for the simple reason that you should find a mirror (full length is best) and practice giving your presentation. You should ensure that you are comfortable with the content (cut and change as required – it is easier here than on stage!) and also that you are interacting with the audience.

Make sure that you are looking up and keeping eye contact with the audience (you, in this case). You should ensure you are not just reading your cue cards. If you are, you need to ensure that you practise using them until they are second nature.

Note – you can replace the mirror with a video camera if you wish, however this can lack the instant feedback you get from looking yourself in the eyes.

In-situ Rehearsals

This is the ultimate luxury, but one you should try to afford yourself. This is to get to the venue early and have a chance to practice on stage with the live presentation.

Mirror rehearsals are great for practice at home before the event; you should ensure you are happy with the content and that you know what you will be speaking about. In-situ rehearsals give you an opportunity to ensure you are comfortable with the venue and equipment. Where will I be standing, how do I move on slides, where do I walk on and off the stage?

Combining the two types of rehearsal will ensure you have both the presentation content and the technology under your control and you will be ready to knock 'em dead!

Section Review

In this section we have started to build our effective presentation. We have:

- learnt the value of preparation, without preparing too much!

- found out about the needs of our audience: who they are and what they want to hear

- asked the crucial questions about the presentation: we know the audience, we are prepared and we read the body language for any issues

- learnt when to ask for questions and how to deal with them

- understood the difference between a script and cue cards

- understood how to rehearse.

Now we will build on these tools to become a perfect presenter!

Become a 'Perfect Presenter'

- Introduction
- Vocal techniques
  - Tone, pitch, projection and inflection
- Harnessing body language
  - Employing an open stance
  - Maintaining eye contact
- Maintaining eye contact
  - Why eye contact is important
  - How to maintain eye contact with a large audience
- Dress to impress
  - Knowing how to dress for your audience
- Section Review

Introduction

Up to this point we have built your presentation skills and given you some techniques to ensure that you are ready and able to give a great presentation. In this section we will take it one step further and build on the skills you have learnt to give you some ways to truly impress your audience.

Vocal Techniques

Do you know what you sound like when you talk? I remember being somewhat shocked when, as a child, I first recorded my voice on a cassette recorder and played it back. We often sound very different from what we hear ourselves. I suggest that you take a presentation or a passage from a book and read it aloud while recording yourself.

Now, what did you hear? And, more importantly, did what you heard sound like someone you would like to listen to for a period of time? By this I mean, did you sound interesting and passionate about what you said or was it more monotone?

Of course, this is not a fair test, but you need to consider how you speak. Verbal communication is vital to any presenter; not only is it essential for you to get your message across, but it can also impart trust and confidence to your audience.

Harnessing Body Language

You have probably heard of the phrase 'body language', and in fact you will be using it subliminally all the time. Body language is the set of non-verbal messages we send; in fact, research says that 80% of our communication is nonverbal and that over 50% is from body language.

Body language portrays how we really feel. A good example is when you are having an argument with someone – if you were to watch their body language you may find that they have their arms crossed, effectively blocking you out.

Using body language as a presenter can be very powerful, particularly using an open stance. This is when you use body language to be open to your audience and take down any barriers. To use an open stance:

- look at how you hold your body – you will likely to be standing when you present, however if you are not, uncross your legs.

- open your arms – use open, slow gestures with your arms, incorporating embracing movements with your palms relaxed towards the audience (don't rapidly wave your fist at the audience, for example!)

- maintain eye contact with your audience – I'll tell you more on the next page!

Body language comes from human beings' very earliest days on the planet, and the open stance works at a very low level in the brain, showing that you are not going to attack the other person and in fact that you are holding yourself open to them.

You should also watch your audience's body language – overall are they responding with open body language or are there many crossed arms showing resistance to you? Are people maintaining your eye contact? In particular look for head nodding, showing direct agreement and subliminally providing positive feedback for you as presenter.

Maintaining Eye Contact

An important part of your body language is maintaining eye contact, you can see this when you are talking with someone one to one. You can very quickly tell if someone is not telling the truth or if they are bored when they do not keep eye contact with you. You can send the same message as a presenter if you do not maintain eye contact with your audience.

Now, of course, if you have a large audience you cannot attempt to look directly at everyone, but you can give the impression that you are. The trick is to select two or three people who are distributed in your audience – for example, if it is a theatre style environment, one or two people on the left hand side and one or two on the right – then, as you speak, look towards these people and try to maintain eye contact, changing the people you look at regularly but not too often. It is good to perhaps glance up from your cue cards and change person or to do so when you change slide.

By doing this there will be groups of the audience who will believe that you are making eye contact with them.

Dress to impress

Part of being a Power Presenter is being in control of your entire environment, this means not just how you are presenting your content, but also how you are presenting yourself.

Before you present you need to be aware of how you should dress. Unfortunately, the days of business dress being a suit and tie for gentlemen and business attire for ladies is now changing, many organisations now have smart causal rules and you can run the risk of turning up and being over- or underdressed for your presentation.

There is an important consideration however, and that is, how would you usually dress for this presentation? The most important thing to remember is that you should be comfortable in your clothes. This is not just in the way they fit, but also how they make you feel. We are trying to build your own confidence and then pass this to the audience, so find clothes that make you feel empowered. Of course you should not turn up in something totally unsuitable (unless that is the impact you wish to make – be careful!) but something that makes you feel right.

They say that clothes maketh the man (or woman!), but it is the confidence with which you wear them that goes much further.

Section Review

In this section we have started to use techniques to develop your presence, voice and body language with your audience. We have:

- understood the importance of good vocal technique

- learnt about body language both as a presenter and how to read your audience

- learnt the importance of eye contact and how to maintain eye contact with a large audience

- understood how to dress as a presenter.

Now we will go on to use storytelling to create a believable and interesting presentation.

Using Storytelling For Presentations

- Introduction

- Why use stories?

- A Poor Presentation

- What lets presentations down

- The Narrative Arc

  - Introduction to the Narrative Arc

  - Presentations as stories

  - Understanding the Narrative Arc

  - The elements of the arc

- Creating a story for your presentation

- Using the Narrative Arc

- Questions to be answered when using the arc

- The Presentation Storyboard

  - Using a storyboard template for your presentations

- ○ Shoot the bullets

- ○ Adding impact with images

- ● Section Review

Introduction

What was the last film you saw? Even if it wasn't all that good, I am sure you could describe the story and tell me the ending. In fact you could probably remember a lot of detail about the whole story.

It's likely that the story involved you and maybe even made you feel happy or sad. No doubt you empathised with the hero and were on the edge of your seat when it looked like the baddies might actually win!

Now, think back to the last presentation you saw – did you feel any emotion? Or were you just dying to get out of the room? Do you remember the ending or any of the detail of the presentation itself? The answer is, unfortunately, probably not.

But why is that?

A poor presentation

We have all seen the familiar presentation slides which are packed full of text, copious bullet points which the speaker is using as their script. It goes to create a boring presentation which will not engage the audience.

It is not a surprise that many presentations are unmemorable. However, it is not just the slides filled with busy text and the poor design that lets most presenters down down. For a presentation to be memorable you need to engage the audience – basically, you need to tell them a story.

The Narrative Arc

The telling of stories goes back many centuries; in fact, it is an ancient tradition which covers everything from cave paintings to Bridget Jones' Diary. We are very familiar with the ways that stories are told and often we come to expect a certain pattern and delivery; this is called the narrative arc:

Understanding the Narrative Arc

You should remember when you give a presentation that, just like a story, there should be a clear beginning, middle and end. Although it may seem complex, the concept of the Narrative Arc is quite simple, it illustrates how we should be bringing the audience from a state where they (effectively) know nothing, through a stage of confrontation where we have to face a number of issues, to a place where their knowledge is higher and there is a clear resolution.

For example, if we split a simple story into the narrative arc:

- Set The Scene Face

- The Issues

- Come To A Resolution

- Meet three pigs

- Pigs build inadequate houses

- Stone House

- Meet wolf (protagonist)

- Wolf starts to blow them down

- Wolf Fricassee

We set the scene, creating a shared introduction before the confrontation, in this case the wolf wanting to eat the pigs before we reach the resolution, happy pigs, unhappy wolf.

You may question how you might use this method with a presentation? Well, we should still have the same steps. For example:

Set The Scene

- Identify the reason for needing a new IT system

Face The Issues

- Getting buy-in from all departments

Come To A Resolution

- Improved customer service

Using the Narrative Arc

Let's be truthful here, we are not expecting you to create a Hollywood blockbuster out of your next presentation, but by using the narrative tools you create something that will be more intuitive to your audience.

To create the narrative arc for a presentation you need to look at the content and ask some questions:

- Why am I here? – This is not the meaning of life, but at least the meaning of the presentation! What do people expect to have achieved by the end of the presentation. This may be certain knowledge, a decision or a call to action.

- Where do I start? – What is the common ground from which you need to start? It is good to start with a question, (for example – why are we not delivering great customer service? Why is our IT system failing?) This should be a common question which your pre-presentation research shows the audience will want to be answered.

- Where do we want to be? – What is the expected resolution?

This should be the outcome for the presentation.

- What are the issues? – What is stopping us reaching the resolution? These are the barriers which we need to overcome and the issues that we need to face.

With this information you should be able to create a presentation storyboard.

Presentation Storyboard

We need to use the narrative arc to create a simple storyboard for your presentation. The storyboard will allow you not only to ensure you cover all of the stages of the arc, but will also allow you to create accurate timings for your presentation.

Shoot the bullets

The other technique you should look at when creating your presentation from the storyboard is to avoid bullet points. Remember:

- the screen is not your script – you have cue cards.

- we don't want to just list the content on the screen for the audience to read. If you do, just ignore the presentation and send them an email.

- a picture says a thousand words.

Instead of pages of bullets which the audience will read ahead of you or just ignore, use photographs, graphics or images.

You can find great photos on the internet from sites such as Pixabay www.pixabay.com which provides many free or cost-effective photos you can use.

Put a photo up on a full screen and do the talking yourself rather than the bullet points. The image should be used to add impact!

Section Review

In this section we reviewed how to use storytelling to create a powerful presentation. We:

- understood why storytelling is important

- learnt about the narrative arc and how to use it for presentations

- gave our presentation a beginning, middle and end

- created a storyboard to build our presentation

- got rid of bullet points to add impact without words.

In the next section you will learn how to deal with anything that could possibly go wrong during your presentation and how to deal with it!

Dealing with problems

Introduction

In a perfect world there would never be any problems: projectors would never break down, people would never ask difficult questions and there would never be any unexpected issues.

Unfortunately, no matter of training and experience can totally prevent problems occurring, however you can certainly take a number of steps to ensure that, if you do encounter an issue, you can manage it without it totally disrupting your presentation.

There are two rules you can use when you have a problem during a presentation, the first is the

NPD rule

NPD = No Permanent Damage

The first rule tells us that we should keep things in perspective. Basically, giving a presentation is considerably less dangerous than a number of other activities (for example: flying a plane, mining or lion taming). We should always remember that, within reason, whatever you do or whatever happens will not cause permanent damage to either you or your audience.

It is worth remembering NPD because you can sometimes feel that the world is about to end when you are giving a presentation and something goes wrong. You are in the spotlight in front of an audience who are all waiting to see how you deal with the situation.

The unexpected can happen to anyone. The difference between the embarrassing moments (for both the audience and the speaker) and memorable moments when something goes wrong are the presenter. You can turn a problem into an opportunity. For example, if the projector fails use this as a chance to show how well you know your subject and just carry on without slides. If you have rehearsed and have your cue cards ready, I can assure you that any audience will forget the problem and be overtaken by admiration with how you dealt with it.

This is when the second rule comes into play...

The PBD Rule

The second rule we need to keep in mind while presenting is the PBD rule:

PBD = Pause, Breathe, Deal with it

Take an example: you are in the middle of a presentation when suddenly the projector stops working – what is your immediate reaction? If it is to panic or become flustered, then this will become obvious for the audience and it will start a spiral of nerves which you may not recover from in the presentation. If it is to immediately and publicly blame the technical staff you will make yourself look bad in the eyes of the audience – I can assure you no technician plans for these things to happen!

What you should do is:

- Pause

  - Take a moment to weigh up the options.

- Breathe

  - If you remember what we said about breathing when dealing with presentation nerves. Taking a deep breath can start to calm you.

- Deal with it

  - You need to carry on or, if that is impossible, take control of the room.

As we said on the last page, you can turn a problem into an opportunity. There is nothing worse than watching a presenter flounder when there is a problem. If you take a moment you can come back stronger than ever!

Dealing with a technology disaster

One of the most common things to go wrong involves technology, and computers in particular! It is all too common to see someone struggling with a computer or tablet moments before a presentation or to have the audience treated to the desktop and a search for the correct file.

The best way to prevent an issue with technology is to prepare before the event and to ensure you have an opportunity to test your presentation and equipment before you have to start speaking. There are a number of common issues which can occur. For example:

- When using your own PC with a projector there is no image displayed.

- When using a supplied PC you find that videos or sound files do not run correctly or that fonts and pictures are incorrect.

Before you give a presentation ensure that you have it backed up on a memory stick or online and ensure that you have saved all the required files (such as video and audio files) as well. If you are using your own laptop make sure you know how to switch on the external monitor output, otherwise the projector will not be able to show your presentation – there is usually a key combination you need to press to get this to work.

Also make sure you go through every slide checking for errors; sometimes different machines can show pictures etc. in different ways. It is important to be sure that diagrams have not been altered and also check that any videos are working (you may need to ask for a sound connection to the public address system and adjust the volume on your machine).If you check all of these items you will eliminate 99% of any issues you may encounter, leaving you with what are mostly very unlikely problems that are out of your hands.

You may want to consider creating a new 'Presentation' user on your device which has no email or other applications. This can be used to deliver presentations with no notifications or annoying pop-ups!

Dealing with difficult people

We have covered preparing for your presentation and ensuring that you have the right content for the audience, however sometimes no matter what you do there will be someone who has another agenda or just wishes to be difficult.

It is very rare that you have to deal with difficult people in a presentation. If you do have to, however, the most important thing to remember is that you have to maintain your Alpha Presenter status. By this I mean that you need to be sure that you do not give control of your audience to the individual.

Firstly, follow the PBD rule: take a breath and respond politely to their issue or concern. Remember that you should listen to their comment when you can (don't allow them to go on, but make an effort to show that you are not just preventing their input). You will need to be forceful but do not try to get into an argument from the lectern. If there is a response you can give do so, if they choose to come back and argue suggest that they take the matter up with you after the presentation. It is impossible to try and have a two- way conversation at the cost of the rest of the audience.

In the most extreme situation when they will not stop arguing you need to stop the presentation until there is order. Apologise to the audience and either blank the screen (hit the B key on your keyboard in PowerPoint to toggle a black screen) or step off the stage. This is extreme; however, it shows that you will not be undermined by the individual.

Remember however that this is a very rare situation and you may never need this advice.

Section Review

In this section we learnt how to deal with issues. We have:

- put problems in perspective with the No Permanent Damage rule

- learnt how to get time to deal with an issue with the Pause, Breathe, Deal with it rule

- learnt how to cope with a technology disaster

- learnt how to deal with difficult people.

In the next section we will look at how you can improve your audience dynamics.

Tools and Techniques to Improve Audience Dynamics

- Introduction
- Using interactive elements
- Breaking the ice
  - Breaking the ice – with small and large groups
- Votes and Polls
- Chat shows and panels
- Debates
- Using music to manage mood
  - Getting the pre-music right
  - Music to build the complete event
  - How to play-out music
  - Being legal with music
- Presentations as theatre

- Ensuring you have the right image

- Perfect presentations – in conclusion

Introduction

You now have tools and techniques which will allow you to prepare and deliver a powerful presentation. This next section discusses how you can take this to an even higher level and really motivate your audience.

Generally, presentations are a one-way delivery method – you speak to your audience and there is generally no interaction in return (with the exception of possible questions and body language).

When you are considering your presentations you should look at how you could possibly look at different ways of working with your audience, particularly if you will be with the same audience all day (for a conference, for example). It may be worth finding different styles to ensure that the audience remain motivated.

There are a variety of techniques which you can use to build audience engagement, for example:

- Icebreakers – activities which are used to enliven an audience and breakdown barriers between individuals and the presenter

- Votes and polls – interactive voting systems which can be used to gauge the audience opinion and input for certain items and can also be used to involve an audience

- Text based interaction – using mobile phone or apps to get live messages during presentations.

There are two particular times when the audience attention is at its lowest and therefore interactive elements can be best employed:

- Opening session – The first presentation of the day has to bridge the void between the long journey to the venue or to wake up a tired audience (from an overexcited night before). Here ice-breakers can be used to wake up an audience and involve them in the presentation.

- The post-lunch slump – One of the times that the audience is least attentive is immediately after lunch. There has been a break from the presentations and also people are digesting food. Here a lively interactive session will keep an audience interested and involved.

Breaking the ice

When you first walk into a conference venue it is likely that you don't know the people around you, or if you do it is in a very different context. Also, you may have had a difficult journey to get to the venue and still be thinking about how you were cut up on a roundabout or the trouble you had finding somewhere to park. Put simply, you are not necessarily in the right mind to get the best from the presentations or to network with the other delegates. It is at this stage that a good icebreaker can be used.

You need to be very careful and this is where knowing your audience from your preparation is important; a good ice-breaker can be great, one that goes badly can damage the whole day. So it is worth thinking about your audience and coming up with a simple idea which can be implemented simply.

Breaking the ice – with small and large groups

If you have a small group of people who do not know each other, an ice-breaker I like to use is 'Truth and Lies'. You ask each delegate to give three points about themselves, two real and one a complete lie. The rest of the delegates have to guess which the lie is. This is a simple ice-breaker; it does not embarrass people as their lie can be simple or as blatant as they wish and you will usually find the lies becoming more colourful as more delegates play the game! This is useful to give a bit of background about the group and it takes away barriers amongst the group.

Of course this is not something which you can replicate in a large audience (unless you have all day!). Here it is better to use a quick and simple activity. For example, 'meet your neighbour' gets audience members to stand up and introduce themselves to the people on the left and right hand side. If your audience does know each other (a company group, for example) you can adapt this into the 'stand up, sit down challenge', where everyone stands up and you ask questions, for example 'sit down if you travelled here by train' until you have only a few people standing. Again you can make the questions as simple or fun according to the audience.

At the end of either icebreaker you should find that the audience is more alive and receptive to your presentations.

Votes and Polls

The use of voting can be a very useful technique for both involving your audience and gaining instant response on important points in your presentation. There are two main techniques which can be used for audience voting:

- Interactive voting systems – You can hire a system which supplies each delegate with a small radio handset (like a television remote control). These are linked into your presentation which means you can ask a question and see displayed an instant result on screen. These systems are very good for accurate results in large audiences and can allow you to ask and display complex questions.

- App based systems - there are low cost apps which can be installed on your audience's devices which can be used for voting and input.

- Digital voting – The cost-free solution is using a digital system. You ask your audience to put their digits in the air (put your hand up). It is a simple and quick way to get an answer to a simple (generally a yes/no) question.

The use of a vote can be useful to allow an audience to give their input to the presentation and this can also increase audience motivation.

It is important to ensure that when you do undertake a vote you are ready to respond to the answer you receive. Even if you are completely sure of the answer you expect, there are times when the anonymous nature of a vote can give you an unexpected result. So do be ready with your response if the answer is the

Yes you expect, but also be ready if the audience give you a No. There is nothing worse than seeing a presenter trying to respond to an unexpected answer. If you expect the unexpected you will be ready for anything!

Chat shows and panels

So far we have really only considered the familiar 'stand up and talk' style of presentation, where you speak to the audience directly. This is often the most suitable method for sharing information with an audience; however, this is certainly not the only way.

Using chat shows, panels and debates allows you to create a more interactive session with your audience as well as breaking up a succession of presentations. In conferences we are no doubt familiar with panel sessions, where you have a selection of speakers at a top table on stage answering audience questions. This can be a very effective technique and will work well if you have followed the steps we highlighted in the section on answering questions from your audience.

An alternative to this method is to change the panel format into a chat show style. In this format, the formality of the top table is replaced with soft seating making the session somewhat more relaxed.

Additionally, you can, if required, carefully script such a session without this being obvious to the audience. If you agree the questions you will be asking you can ensure that your 'guest' is ready with an answer.

The chat show ensures that you give the impression of an interactive session but does not depend on questions coming directly from the audience. It can be structured to meet the aims and objectives of the session and has the strong advantage of being a format which is very familiar with the audience.

Debates

The last and perhaps most challenging and exciting format is the debate. Here, you can encourage your audience to consider two (or more) different contrary views and is well placed before lunch or coffee when the audience can discuss the points raised outside of the conference.

You need to be careful with the development of a debate. You need two strong and confident speakers, as you do not want one side of the argument to collapse without delivering their point. Additionally, you need to be sure of what subjects you wish to cover and have a good contrary argument. For example:

- We need to hold more physical meetings with our members vs. We need to use more electronic meeting technology

- Customer service is more important than IT systems vs. IT

- Systems are more important than customer service

- Our industry is on the brink of decline vs. Our industry is on the brink of success

Each of the debate topics above illustrate the need for a relevant topic that is of interest to the audience and that the audience is likely to have a view on. The subject can certainly be controversial, however you need to ensure that overall you reach a conclusion which meets the aims for the event (don't just court controversy for no reason, there must be a purpose).

To manage a debate you should give each speaker an equal amount of time (carefully and strictly enforced) and have a chairperson who can sum up the points raised in conclusion for each speaker. Short, sharp speeches are best (think of the US Presidential debates). Five minutes without PowerPoint will be more memorable and will force the points to be made clearly and concisely.

As you close a debate you can use a vote to show where the audience stands or you may wish to encourage conversation during a break, however it is important to close the discussion with a sound conclusion.

Using music to manage mood

Earlier in the book we discussed music and how this could change your mood as a presenter. If you remember we said that a good, upbeat track could leave you feeling energised and alive. I told you that you should find a track that did this for you and play it before you go out to speak. Following this concept, there is no reason why we do not use the same technique to enliven your audience.

If you think back to our example of film, can you remember the last film that started without a theme tune? The music is used to set the scene and prepare us for what is following, however how often do you go to a conference or presentation and wait in silence before the presenter steps out to speak?

There are two types of music you should consider: pre-flight and walk- on.

- Pre-flight – This is music which is playing in the background before the event starts. Do resist too much 'test card' music or slow light classical in preference for more upbeat music.

- Walk-on – This is your theme tune. This is a short piece of music (30 seconds or less) which should be used whenever there is a change of presenter or end of session. It should again be upbeat and played louder than the pre-flight music.

- The walk-on is the 'stop talking we are about to start' music and is used to make people concentrate on the stage and the presentation.

You can find a number of ways to run music. If you have the luxury of having a sound engineer, they can play music and change tracks when you are ready to start. If instead you need to run the whole show from your laptop you can embed music in your presentation software. Use the following steps:

1. Set up a slide which plays a selection of music tracks for pre- flight.

2. Create a second title slide which has your walk-on music embedded and set to play automatically when you open the slide.

3. When you are ready to start the show just wait for the end of a track (and the nice fade-out it provides) and click on your remote radio mouse to trigger the walk-on music and your title slide.

It is important to give your event a theme; you can do this by using the walk-on music whenever a session starts or ends (in the same way television programmes use theme music at the beginning, end and whenever there is a break). In this way your audience will not only feel the event is more professional, but it gives them cues to know when sessions are starting and finishing.

Being legal with music

Of course you need to be careful when you play music in public as there are licensing requirements from organisations such as the Performing Rights Society (PRS). The PRS are responsible for ensuring that musicians are paid when their music is used.

You will find that most conference venues (hotels and conference centres, for example) are already licensed, but you must ensure that you check with the venue before you play copyright music. If you are using your own premises you either need to obtain a licence or use royalty-free music. It is important to realise that licensing will only cover the use of the music for play-out at your event and there will be additional requirements if, for example, you wish to video or transmit the proceedings for example. Again, royalty-free music may be the best solution.

Royalty-free music is music which you purchase with rights for you to use (according to the specific licence you purchase) for use at events and for video or transmission. There are a number of providers of royalty-free music available on the Internet and you can find very cost- effective music which can be selected to best suit your event.

Events as theatre – Image is everything

Imagine the scene: you have gone to the theatre and half way through the show someone steps up stopping the action while they adjust some of the set. There is a pause for a few minutes while the audience wait in silence before the next act finally starts.

If this happened, you would have every right to be disappointed. The whole idea of theatre is that we attend to see a professional show in order that we are totally immersed in the content; if we see how the show works it ruins the illusion.

The same is true when you see someone changing laptops in front of the audience or struggling with the presentation software trying to load the right file. We all know that a laptop is being used, we know how the presentation is being done, however we don't want to see the workings! The moment that an audience sees this, any effort you have put into creating a professional image is destroyed.

It sounds like a simple mistake; however, it has a major impact on the way the audience thinks of the presenter (your Alpha Presenter status is immediately damaged). People will presume that you have failed to prepare or rehearse for your presentation and that you are clearly not ready.

Ensuring you have the right image

There are some simple rules you can employ to ensure that you do not damage the image of presenters and maintain the 'theatre' of your presentation:

1. Don't use the words presentation or event – think show!

○ If you think of your event as a show you will start to recognise that it is more than just a collection of presentations. You should be looking to enthral and involve your audience just as you would if you went to the theatre.

2. Be ready

○ Have all of the presentations ready, loaded and tested well ahead of the show. This means that rule 3 must be adhered to.

3. No changes on show day

○ How often do you get the request 'just to change one thing' or 'I have a new version on this memory stick'. Unless you are very careful you can replace your checked and rehearsed version with a version which you do not know. You have to say that you will not make changes or accept new versions after you have completed your checks.

4. The stage is not a public place

   - You would not expect anyone but actors on a theatre stage, so don't allow anyone but speakers on the stage during your show. I know it sounds petty, but people moving about on stage can distract the audience from the presentation.

5. Never show the application or the desktop

   - You can easily create a file which embeds an entire day's presentations, therefore you don't need to switch between files or load the application. Save presentations as show files and have them loaded and ready before the audience come in. If you must have a second laptop in use, ask your technicians to provide a 'switcher' which will allow you to have two laptops and switch smoothly between them without struggling with projector leads.

Perfect presentations – in conclusion

If you follow the simple rules and techniques I have set out you will create presentations which will allow you to ensure your message is delivered effectively. You should speak with confidence and conviction and truly capture your audience.

You can distil this entire section of the book into a few points:

• Know what to say – Know what your audience want to listen to, understand your topic and be rehearsed and ready.

• Be ready for anything – Prepare and ensure you remove any possible things that could go wrong and then put anything that does in perspective and deal with it.

• Think like a film – Use the narrative arc to create a story for your presentation. This is a technique which we are all familiar with and understand.

• Create a show – Keep everything slick and professional to ensure that your audience are impressed and concentrate on the content without being distracted by simple errors.

Good luck with your next show!

www.ingramcontent.com/pod-product-compliance
Lightning Source LLC
Chambersburg PA
CBHW070105210526
45170CB00013B/747